JOURNEYBOOK

JOURNEYBOOK

A Guided Travel Journal and Trip Planner to Inspire and Facilitate Your Travels

UB Hawthorn

THE MINDFUL WORD
www.themindfulword.org

Visit us at www.themindfulword.org

The Mindful Word
701-1120 Finch Ave. W. #928
Toronto, Ontario
M3J 3H7, Canada

ISBN 978-0-9939566-0-7

Printed in the United States of America

Twenty years from now you will be more disappointed by the things that you didn't do than by the ones you did do. So throw off the bowlines. Sail away from the safe harbour. Catch the trade winds in your sails. Explore. Dream. Discover.
MARK TWAIN

CONTENTS

Few experiences in life can captivate us with the intensity of travel. All at the same time, travel can activate the senses, engage the mind, spark powerful feelings and tap into the soul.

Whether it's seeing a mighty African elephant for the first time, wandering in rapture through a cathedral in Florence or listening to the hypnotic hum of Tibetan monks chanting there's a lot to absorb when travelling. A little bit too much sometimes to really make something out of it.

Enter the journal. Taking the time to ponder the many goings on of the day gives us an opportunity to make sense of what we experienced. By reflecting on our experiences we can deepen our connection to a place we visit, the people we meet and the things we do, making travel that much more powerful.

Use the Trip Planner to assist with all the practicalities of travel like packing and budgeting. This section offers checklists, itineraries and other practical tools to guide you through all the quirks of travel planning.

The Travel Journal section offers a number of tips and writing prompts to help you develop a regular routine of journal writing, and inspirational quotes are included along the way to keep you engaged as you jot down your memories.

Travelling brings up questions. A lot of them. The Travel Resources section provides tools to answer some of your questions as well as a list of online resources to point you in the right direction.

Travel forces us to grow in ways that we likely would not if we stayed on home turf and failed to push our boundaries. Just as a seed grows into a mighty tree, we can use travel to plant a seed of potential. Experience it. Feel it. Absorb it… then reflect on it and record it here.

TRIP PLANNER

When preparing to travel, lay out all your
clothes and all your money. Then take
half the clothes and twice the money.
SUSAN HELLER

BEFORE YOU GO CHECKLIST

One to three months before

☐   **Get visas for the countries you're visiting**
During peak travel times (Spring break, summer and winter holidays) allow for more time to obtain visas.

☐   **Visit a travel doctor**
Find out what vaccinations are necessary (some countries demand that you have certain vaccinations or else they won't let you in). Do your research because not all vaccinations proposed by the doctor will be necessary and some have significant side effects. Spread your vaccinations out so you're not getting them all at once to minimize the impact on your body.

☐   **Check your passport expiration date**
Apply for a new passport if it's expiring soon. Some countries require that your passport remain valid for six months or else they won't let you in!

☐   **Plan out your activities**
Search for things you'd like to see and do in guidebooks or online (refer to the Travel Resources section for good sources).

☐   **Book it**
Book transportation and reserve tours, guides and sightseeing activities. Tip: students can look into getting an ISIC card for discounts. Seniors, families and other special groups may also be eligible for reduced rates.

☐   **Learn the local language**
Read books, take courses or listen to audio files (see the Travel Resources at the back for some ideas on the best ways to learn a language).

One to two weeks before

☐ **Call your credit card company and bank**
Let them know you're travelling and for how long. When they see purchases being made out of country their fraud departments tend to put a hold on credit cards. Also, ask about international plans in which you can use your ATM card abroad without having to pay withdrawal fees.

☐ **Look into travel insurance**
If you already have an insurance plan or credit card you may already be covered for travel, so call them up and inquire. If you're not covered, consider buying travel insurance for trip cancellation and medical (refer to the Travel Resources section).

☐ **Arrange pet care**
Ask a friend to care for your pets or arrange a pet sitter to stay at your home. You can also find a lodging facility, kennel or boarding host to care for your pets while you're away.

☐ **Read up on local customs and culture**
Doing this is not just a good idea to better appreciate the place you're visiting, but necessary in some instances to avoid potential problems (i.e. knowing to cover the body in countries where the people dress conservatively).

☐ **Take passport photos**
Take some extra passport photos if you're planning on setting up a SIM card, joining programs or getting visas and permits while on your trip. Even if you don't use the photos they can be nice to give away to travellers and locals you meet along the way.

☐ **Make photocopies or scan**
Photocopy your passport, visa, immunization records and other important documents. Store them separately from the originals. You can also back them up on a device and in the cloud.

In the week before

☐   **Sign up for a mobile phone plan**
Find a plan that provides coverage where you're going. Alternatively, unlock your phone and get a SIM upon arriving at your destination—it could be a lot cheaper than roaming.

☐   **Cancel / hold services**
Cancel or put your newspaper delivery and other services on hold.

☐   **Prepaid billing**
Sign up for prepaid billing for your mobile, Internet and other bills if you haven't done so already.

☐   **Print out your plane and other tickets**
If these can be downloaded digitally, you can save the paper and hassle by doing it this way. Just make sure your mobile has power when you need it! As a backup you could download the tickets to a second device.

☐   **Keep connected**
Write up a copy of your itinerary for a family member or friend so they know where you're going. Also, sign up with your country's Foreign Affairs ministry to receive travel alerts in the country you're visiting (e.g. tsunami or civil unrest) as well as to inform them of your whereabouts in case there's an emergency.

☐   **Check the weather**
Find out the short-term and long-term forecasts for your destination so you'll have a better idea of what to pack.

☐   **Pack**
Refer to the Packing Checklist later in this section. Be aware of any prohibited items that you can't bring onto a plane, such as sharp objects and flammables.

Departure day

☐ **Dress right**
Planes, buses and trains can get cool so it's good to have an extra layer and a rain jacket handy in case it pours. And make sure to dress comfortably!

☐ **Have everything?**
Check that you have everything and that the things you need to carry with you are in your carry-on, not your packed luggage (refer to the Packing Checklist).

☐ **Arrive early**
Arrive at the airport early, especially if you're flying internationally. If taking a bus or train it doesn't require as much time, but either way it's nice to not have to rush.

PACKING CHECKLIST

CLOTHES

☐ Shirts

☐ Pants / skirts

☐ Underwear

☐ Socks / stockings

☐ Swimsuit

☐ Coat

☐ Pajamas / sleepwear

☐ Winter hat / scarf / gloves

☐ Belts

☐ Dresses

☐

☐

☐ T-shirts

☐ Sweaters / sweatshirts

☐ Bras / undershirts

☐ Shorts

☐ Sun hat / visor / cap

☐ Rain jacket

☐ Shoes / sandals

☐ Thermal underwear

☐ Ties

☐ Suits

☐

☐

CARRY-ON

☐ Books / ebooks

☐ Cash / cards

☐ Keys

☐ Flight / train / bus tickets

☐ Insurance documents

☐ Photocopy of passport

☐ Medication / birth control

☐ Earplugs

☐ Guidebook / map

☐ Water bottle

☐ Change of clothes

☐ Travel pillow / blanket

☐ Journal

☐

☐

☐ Mobile

☐ Passport / ID

☐ Laptop / tablet

☐ Itinerary / directions

☐ Medical records

☐ Vitamins / supplements

☐ Pain relievers / Gravol

☐ Eye mask

☐ Batteries / memory card

☐ Snacks

☐ Camera

☐ Kleenex

☐ Pen/pencil

☐

☐

TOILETRIES

- ☐ Toothbrush
- ☐ Dental floss
- ☐ Shampoo
- ☐ Soap / gel / cleanser
- ☐ Moisturizing lotion
- ☐ Makeup / remover
- ☐ Q-tips / cotton
- ☐ Nail clippers / file
- ☐ Feminine hygiene products
- ☐ Contact lenses / solution
- ☐ Hand sanitizer
- ☐
- ☐
- ☐ Toothpaste
- ☐ Mouthwash
- ☐ Conditioner
- ☐ Comb / brush
- ☐ Suntan lotion
- ☐ Deodorant
- ☐ Chapstick
- ☐ Tweezers
- ☐ Shaving supplies
- ☐ Bandages
- ☐ Insect repellent
- ☐
- ☐

OTHER

- ☐ Travel adapter
- ☐ Mobile / laptop chargers
- ☐ Luggage tags
- ☐ Sewing kit
- ☐ Money belt
- ☐ Bandana / handkerchief
- ☐ Combination lock
- ☐
- ☐
- ☐ Glasses / sunglasses
- ☐ Emergency contact list
- ☐ Copies of passport/ cards
- ☐ First aid kit
- ☐ Extra batteries
- ☐ Extra bag / laundry bag
- ☐ Water purification
- ☐
- ☐

TEN ESSENTIALS (primarily for outdoor trips)

- ☐ Map and compass
- ☐ Insulation (extra clothes)
- ☐ First aid kit
- ☐ Repair kit / tools
- ☐ Extra water
- ☐ Sunglasses / sunscreen
- ☐ Headlamp / flashlight
- ☐ Matches / lighter / candle
- ☐ Extra food
- ☐ Emergency shelter

9

TRAVEL IDEAS

Use this space to set your intention for your travels or if you'd like to plan it out, you can record prices, websites, phone numbers and contact information so you can reference it later as you're narrowing down your options. If you've collected articles from travel magazines, glue or staple them in.

THE VISION

Briefly sketch out the trip you want. Where you want to go, what you really want to do and learn, why you're going, who you're going with, when you're going. Then in the following sections you can get into the specifics as to how you'll make it all happen.

ACCOMMODATION
Hotels, B&Bs, Hostels, Camping, Agritourism

TRANSPORTATION

Flights, Trains, Buses, Car Rentals, Hiking, Biking,
Motorcycling, Cruises

SIGHTSEEING

Attractions, Tours, Museums, Art Galleries, Gardens,
Monuments, Parks, Historic Sites, Religious Sites

FOOD, DRINK & ENTERTAINMENT
Restaurants, Bars, Nightclubs, Sports, Concerts, Festivals, Performances

VISA CHECKLIST

Country	Visa require-ments	Visa length / How long to get visa	Cost of visa	Other notes

TRAVEL BUDGET

Expense	Budget	Actual	Difference
Transportation			
Flights			
Trains			
Buses			
Taxis			
Car rentals			
Gas			
Road tolls			
Accommodation / Food			
Hotel			
B&B			
Hostel			
Camping			
Breakfast			
Lunch			
Dinner			
Snacks			
Entertainment / Shopping			
Tours			
Tickets			
Entertainment			
Gifts			
Other			
Insurance			
Immunizations			
TOTAL			

ITINERARY
Overview

Date	Location	Transport	Notes

ITINERARY
Detailed

Day: _____ Location: _____

_____

_____

_____

Day: _____ Location: _____

_____

_____

_____

Day: _____ Location: _____

_____

_____

_____

Day: _____ Location: _____

_____

_____

_____

Day: _____ Location: _____

_____

_____

_____

Day: _____ Location: _____

_____

_____

_____

Day: _____ Location: _____

_____

_____

_____

Day: _____ Location: _____

_____

_____

_____

Day: _____ Location: _____

_____

_____

_____

Day: _____ Location: _____

_____

_____

_____

Every day is a journey, and the journey itself is home.
MATSUO BASHO

Day: _____ Location: _____

_____

_____

_____

Day: _____ Location: _____

_____

_____

_____

Day: _____ Location: _____

_____

_____

_____

Day: _____ Location: _____

_____

_____

_____

Day: _____ Location: _____

_____

_____

_____

Wherever you go, go with all your heart.
CONFUCIUS

Day: _____ Location: _____

_____

_____

_____

Day: _____ Location: _____

_____

_____

_____

Day: _____ Location: _____

_____

_____

_____

Day: _____ Location: _____

_____

_____

_____

Day: _____ Location: _____

_____

_____

_____

Make voyages. Attempt them... there's nothing else.
TENNESSEE WILLIAMS

Day: _____ Location/Transportation: _____

_____

_____

_____

Day: _____ Location/Transportation: _____

_____

_____

_____

Day: _____ Location/Transportation: _____

_____

_____

_____

Day: _____ Location/Transportation: _____

_____

_____

_____

Day: _____ Location/Transportation: _____

_____

_____

_____

Life is either a daring adventure or nothing at all.
HELEN KELLER

23

TRAVEL JOURNAL

Perhaps travel cannot prevent bigotry, but by
demonstrating that all peoples cry, laugh, eat, worry
and die, it can introduce the idea that if we try and
understand each other, we may even become friends.
MAYA ANGELOU

Travel can be a transformative experience. Through journaling and taking the time to draw inward and reflect on your experiences, you can derive greater meaning from your trip and better insight into who you are.

Journal writing also helps us recall things we otherwise would have forgotten and preserves them as memories to forever look back on. And you'll find that journaling opens you up to new ways of experiencing a place. You'll become more aware and alert as you train your senses to more keenly pick up on stimuli.

Journal your travels in the following pages. Though some tips are listed below, there's no prescribed way to journal—do whatever works best for you!

JOURNAL WRITING TIPS

Record the memorable stuff – Though one part of journaling is to record details that you can refer to later, like the exact location of a hard-to-find little beach, giving a play-by-play account of your entire trip can turn the task into a chore. Instead, try focusing on the most memorable experiences and then reflecting on those. The important thing is to write with inspiration.

Use all your senses – Record what all your senses pick up: sight, smell, hearing, touch, taste. Avoid relying on your dominant sense by focusing on what your other senses picked up. You can try a day or two of just writing about what you smelled or what you heard.

Reflect on your experiences – Use your journaling time as your reflection time. It's easy to get caught up with the fast pace of a trip and end up missing out on the important reflection time. So try to set aside a little bit of time every day to journal. Here are some questions you can ask yourself: What did you learn from your experience? What surprised you? How did you feel? What judgments did you make?

Pick up on trends and themes – Are your new surroundings causing you to think and act in a certain way? For better or worse? Have you noticed any change since you started the trip or have you been acting the same way consistently? What do you make of it?

Show don't tell – Don't just describe a scene with boring adjectives. Relive the scene by writing out the actual dialogue that you heard and a few telling details about each experience like that hunchbacked centenarian riding his camel down the middle of an eight-lane road during rush hour with cars and motorcycles whizzing by him at 80 kph—paint a vivid picture!

Illustrate your journey – Don't just rely on words to depict your travels. Draw a picture of that funky bird you saw or sketch in a memorable sunset. You can also keep mementos of your journey by gluing or stapling in train tickets, newspaper snippets and other items of interest. The last 10 pages of the Travel Journal are left blank for this purpose.

Journal while it's fresh – The best time to journal is right after you've had a thrilling experience, when you're still charged and itching to relive it. At this time you'll not just write better and more enthusiastically, but your recollection of events and details will be better.

Give thanks – Travel opens our eyes to a different world that can oftentimes be difficult. Journaling is one way to express our gratitude for what we have.

Let it flow – Though journaling is a time for reflection, it's also a time for expression, so try writing whatever comes to your mind and seeing where it takes you.

WRITING PROMPTS

Even the hardest of the hardcore travel journal writers need some extra kick now and then to get writing. Here are a few prompts you can use as starting off points when writing about a specific day or reflecting on your trip in general...

☐ What was the first thought that came into your head when you arrived at your destination?

☐ What was the one thing you did today that you would most like to remember 20 years from now?

☐ What was the single most sensory stimulating thing you saw (or heard, smelled, touched, tasted)?

☐ Who did you meet today and what will you remember about that encounter?

☐ What was the funniest thing you experienced today?

☐ How are you getting along with your travel mates (or if alone, yourself)?

☐ Why are you travelling?

☐ How do you feel today?

☐ Did you witness something emotionally moving? How did you react at the time and how do you feel now?

☐ Draw a basic map of the area you're staying in and mark down any favourite places you've eaten, landmarks, interesting sights you've seen, etc.

☐ Where are you going next and why?

☐ What's the most interesting expression you've found in the local culture? Or phrase, custom, gesture, etc.

☐ What have you learned so far on your trip?

☐ Has there been one thought that keeps on running through your head on this trip?

☐ What's the most amazing or surprising thing you've noticed about the local people, place or culture?

☐ What's the most difficult thing to understand about the local culture or customs and what's your understanding of it (if any)?

☐ Name one common thing in your new environment and explain its relevance.

☐ Could you live here? If yes, why? If no, why not?

☐ Have you changed since starting your trip? If so, how?

☐ What's your favourite/least favourite local food so far?

☐ Sketch out a picture of an interesting bird or other animal you saw today.

☐ What's the most memorable place you've stayed and why?

☐ And here's a good one to start off the trip: List all judgments, preconceptions, beliefs and stereotypes you have about the people and place you're visiting. After writing them out put them in a box and toss it away. Enjoy your trip!

Experience, travel—these are as education in themselves.
EURIPIDES

A traveller without observation is a bird without wings.
MOSLIH EDDIN SAADI

A ship in harbour is safe, but that
is not what ships are built for.
JOHN A. SHEDD

He who is outside his door has the hardest
part of his journey behind him.
DUTCH PROVERB

Travel teaches toleration.
BENJAMIN DISRAELI

To awaken quite alone in a strange town is
one of the pleasantest sensations in the world.
FREYA STARK

If all difficulties were known at the outset of a long journey,
most of us would never start out at all.
DAN RATHER

Don't tell me how educated you are,
tell me how much you travelled.
MOHAMMED

The first condition of understanding
a foreign country is to smell it.
RUDYARD KIPLING

The use of travelling is to regulate imagination
by reality, and instead of thinking how things
may be, to see them as they are.
SAMUEL JOHNSON

We are all travellers in the wilderness of this world, and the best
we can find in our travels is an honest friend.
ROBERT LOUIS STEVENSON

Travel penetrates your consciousness, but not in a rational way.
MILTON GLASER

Travel far enough, you meet yourself.
DAVID MITCHELL

The traveller sees what he sees, the
tourist sees what he has come to see.
GILBERT K. CHESTERTON

A good traveller is one who does not know
where he is going to, and a perfect traveller
does not know where he came from.
LIN YUTANG

You know more of a road by having travelled it than by all
the conjectures and descriptions in the world.
WILLIAM HAZLITT

Own only what you can always carry with you:
know languages, know countries, know people. Let your
memory be your travel bag.
ALEKSANDR SOLZHENITSYN

Wherever you go becomes a part of you somehow.
ANITA DESAI

I have found out that there ain't no surer
way to find out whether you like people
or hate them than to travel with them.
MARK TWAIN

I dislike feeling at home when I am abroad.
GEORGE BERNARD SHAW

All journeys have secret destinations
of which the traveller is unaware.
MARTIN BUBER

Not all those who wander are lost.
J.R.R. TOLKIEN

I tramp a perpetual journey.
WALT WHITMAN

Certainly, travel is more than the seeing
of sights; it is a change that goes on, deep
and permanent, in the ideas of living.
MARY RITTER BEARD

I never travel without my diary. One should always have
something sensational to read in the train.
OSCAR WILDE

A journey is like marriage. The certain way
to be wrong is to think you control it.
JOHN STEINBECK

I see my path, but I don't know where
it leads. Not knowing where I'm going is
what inspires me to travel it.
ROSALIA DE CASTRO

To travel is to discover that everyone
is wrong about other countries.
ALDOUS HUXLEY

To travel is to take a journey into yourself.
DANNY KAYE

Bizarre travel plans are dancing lessons from God.
KURT VONNEGUT

One travels more usefully when
alone, because he reflects more.
THOMAS JEFFERSON

Freedom is something that dies unless it's used.
HUNTER S. THOMPSON

Travel is the only thing you buy that makes you richer.
UNKNOWN

Once the travel bug bites there is no
known antidote, and I know that I shall be
happily infected until the end of my life.
MICHAEL PALIN

Travel makes one modest. You see what a
tiny place you occupy in the world.
GUSTAVE FLAUBERT

If you reject the food, ignore the customs, fear the religion and avoid the people, you might better stay home.
JAMES MICHENER

Every dreamer knows that it is entirely possible to be
homesick for a place you've never been to, perhaps
more homesick than for familiar ground.
JUDITH THURMAN

The more I travelled the more I realized that fear makes
strangers of people who should be friends.
SHIRLEY MACLAINE

Travellers never think that they are the foreigners.
MASON COOLEY

I don't know where i am going but I'm on my way.
CARL SAGAN

A good traveller has no fixed plans,
and is not intent on arriving.
LAO TZU

Like all great travellers, I have seen more than I remember,
and remember more than I have seen.
BENJAMIN DISRAELI

Wandering re-establishes the original harmony which once
existed between man and the universe.
ANATOLE FRANCE

If you wish to travel far and fast, travel
light. Take off all your envies, jealousies,
unforgiveness, selfishness and fears.
CESARE PAVESE

When you travel, remember that a foreign country
is not designed to make you comfortable. It is
designed to make its own people comfortable.
CLIFTON FADIMAN

Travel can be one of the most
rewarding forms of introspection.
LAWRENCE DURRELL

One doesn't discover new lands without consenting
to lose sight of the shore for a very long time.
ANDRÉ GIDE

Long-term travel doesn't require a massive bundle
of cash; it requires only that we walk through the
world in a more deliberate way.
ROLF POTTS

All travel has its advantages. If the passenger visits better countries, he may learn to improve his own. And if fortune carries him to worse, he may learn to enjoy it.
SAMUEL JOHNSON

The ideal is to feel at home anywhere, everywhere.
GEOFF DYE

TRAVEL RESOURCES

The real voyage of discovery consists not in
seeking new landscapes but in having new eyes.
MARCEL PROUST

WORLD MAP

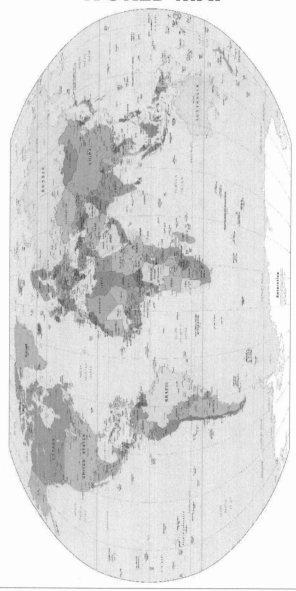

TIME ZONES MAP

TIME ZONE LIST
(Standard time)

Western Hemisphere

GMT -12: Baker Island, Mid-Pacific
GMT -11: Midway Island, American Samoa
GMT -10: Honolulu, Cook Islands
GMT -9: Anchorage, Juneau, French Polynesia
GMT -8: Los Angeles, Vancouver, Seattle, Tijuana
GMT -7: Calgary, Denver, Phoenix, Santa Fe, Mazatlan
GMT -6: Chicago, Dallas, Guatemala, Mexico City
GMT -5: New York, Toronto, Washington, Bogota, Lima
GMT -4: Santiago, La Paz, Asuncion, San Juan, Halifax
GMT -3: Buenos Aires, Montevideo, Rio de Janeiro
GMT -2: Fernando de Noronha, Mid-Atlantic
GMT -1: Azores, Cape Verde

Eastern Hemisphere

GMT 0: London, Lisbon, Dublin, Tangier, Reykjavik
GMT +1: Paris, Rome, Berlin, Prague, Kinshasa, Lagos
GMT +2: Beirut, Athens, Cairo, Cape Town, Tel Aviv
GMT +3: Addis Ababa, Kampala, Nairobi, Mecca, Minsk
GMT +4: Moscow, St. Petersburg, Tbilisi, Abu Dhabi
GMT +5: Karachi, Lahore, Tashkent, Dushanbe, Male
GMT +6: Dhaka, Astana, Thimphu, Perm, Bishkek
GMT +7: Bangkok, Jakarta, Phnom Penh, Ho Chi Minh
GMT +8: Beijing, Shanghai, Hong Kong, Manila, Perth
GMT +9: Tokyo, Osaka, Seoul, Irkutsk, Ambon, Dili
GMT +10: Sydney, Brisbane, Guam, Port Moresby
GMT +11: Vladivostok, Micronesia, Solomon Islands
GMT +12: Auckland, Wellington, Fiji, Tuvalu, Nauru

CONVERSION TABLE

UNIT	SYMBOL	DEFINITION	SI UNITS
cup	C	8 US fl oz ≡ 1/16 gal	236.588 mL
foot	Ft	0.3048 m ≡ 1/3 yd ≡ 12 inches	0.3048 m
gallon	Gal	231 cu in	3.78541 L
inch	In	2.54 cm ≡ 1/36 yd ≡ 1/12 ft	0.0254 m
mile	Mi	5,280 ft ≡ 1,760 yd	1,609.344 m
mile per hour	Mph	1.6093 kph	1.6093 kph
nautical mile	NM; nmi	1,852 m	1,852 m
ounce	Oz	28 g (mass) 30 mL (volume)	28 g (mass) 30 mL (volume)
pint	Pt	⅛ gal (US)	473.176 mL
pound	Lb	0.453592 kg	0.453592 kg
quart	Qt	¼ gal	946.353 mL
yard	Yd	≡ 0.9144 m ≡ 3 ft ≡ 36 in	≡ 0.9144 m

USEFUL WEBSITES AND APPS

Booking

Hotwire – Booking site focused on cheap and discount travel for flights, hotels, cars and vacations. (*www.hotwire.com*)

Last Minute Travel – If booking last minute isn't a problem for you, check out the deals and coupons on this site for accommodation, transportation, holidays and travel activities. (*www.lastminutetravel.com*)

Responsibletravel.com – This tour booking site promises holidays that care about local communities, culture, wildlife conservation and the environment. They ensure this by asking accommodation and tour operators to promise to a set of guidelines and they monitor their operations through traveller reviews. (*www.responsibletravel.com*)

Priceline – An alternative approach to booking where you bid a price and if the place you're bidding on agrees to your price you get it. (*www.priceline.com*)

Booking.com – Billed as the world's #1 accommodation site, they guarantee the best prices on anything from campsites to luxury hotels. (*www.booking.com*)

Expedia – Another option for booking that offers a wide range of options along with reviews. (*www.expedia.com*)

Kayak – Save yourself some time by comparing prices from hundreds of travel sites in one search. (*www.kayak.com*)

The Man in Seat Sixty-One – This man knows a heck of a lot about overland travel. Get detailed information on train, bus and boat trips, including long and complex routes, along with links to sites where you can book your tickets. (*www.seat61.com*)

G Adventures – "The Great Adventure People" deliver tours across a full spectrum to suit different travellers: young adults, families, rail tours, marine tours, etc. (*www.gadventures.com*)

Cruise Sheet – Pick up a good deal on a cruise with some selling for less than $25 a day. (*www.cruisesheet.com*)

Travel Sharing / Home Exchange

Easynest – Useful for solo travellers, this site lets users post their hotel rooms so they can split the cost with another traveller. If you're OK with having a roommate you cut the price of a room in half. (*www.easynest.com*)

FlightCar – Rather than pay huge rates to park your car at the airport why not rent it out and make some cash? This site does just that, facilitating the rental of your car to approved travelling members. (*flightcar.com*)

Airbnb – Search for a room, condo, house or other accommodation from the worldwide network of Airbnb hosts who put their home up for rent. (*www.airbnb.com*)

HomeExchange – Similar to Airbnb, this site offers a fully functional free trial, unlimited exchanges and free listings with a paid membership. (*www.homeexchange.com*)

9flats.com – Another home exchange site with a good selection of listings. (*www.9flats.com*)

Guides / Trip Planning

Wikivoyage – The same foundation that runs Wikipedia does it again, this time with a travel focus. Like all wikis this site is open to users to write and edit content. Unlike traditional travel guides it has the potential to go deeper and cover more because there are so many users working on it. (*www.wikivoyage.org*)

Lonely Planet – A trusted name for travel guides, Lonely Planet is the most successful travel publisher with over 100 million copies sold in over 40 years. The Lonely Planet website builds on the experience and following of the LP brand, offering articles, tours, booking and a high-traffic forum, Thorn Tree, where travellers can offer and receive advice. (*www.lonelyplanet.com*)

Frommer's – This guide book publisher's website features informative travel tips and tools as well as trip ideas, hotels, destinations and a forum. (*www.frommers.com*)

Tripit – This travel planning app gathers all your flights, hotel bookings and whatever other plans you add to it and keeps track of it for you. It can pull booking confirmations directly from your email account or you can add them manually or forward the confirmation emails to Tripit. It also supports team travel so you can coordinate where everyone in your group is and at what time. (*www.tripit.com*)

Viator – A travel booking site specifically for tours and activities. Viator bills itself as a site for insider travelling because they pre-vet all the tours they list and they also have verified reviews and photos to make sure that you make the right decision. (*www.viator.com*)

Vayable – From walking tours to wine tastings, you can hire local guides to show you around or even list your own tours and earn money as a travel guide. (*www.vayable.com*)

Accommodation

Couchsurfing – Enter the sharing economy as a Couchsurfer or a host. Hosts make couches available in their home, usually for a short period of time. It's a nice exchange where the host and traveller get to share travel stories and build a connection. It's also nice to meet locals to introduce you to a new place. (*www.couchsurfing.org*)

Hostelworld – A booking site specifically for finding hostels. Their rating system is particularly helpful since many hostels can be quite dodgy. (*www.hostelworld.com*)

Agriturismo – Italy is known for a particular kind of tourism called agriturismo, a rural vacation where you enjoy a relaxing time immersed in nature on the farm, (*www.agriturismo.it*)

Farm Stay U.S. – An equivalent to agriturismo is a farm stay. Search this site for farms in the U.S. (*www.farmstayus.com*)

Reserve America – Whether you're camping, RVing or just looking for a cozy cabin to settle in for a restful retreat, you can use this site to locate a suitable campground with all the amenities you need. (*www.reserveamerica.com*)

Travel Alerts

U.S. Department of State Alerts and Warnings – This site provides up-to-date travel warnings to advise you what to watch out for wherever you're travelling. (*travel.state.gov*)

Travel Ideas

WWOOF – Worldwide Opportunities on Organic Farms is an organization that links volunteers with farms. In exchange for working about four to six hours a day, farms provide free accommodation and food. This is a great alternative for travellers wanting to gain some hands-on agricultural skills while meeting new people and gaining unique experiences. (*www.wwoof.net*)

Verge Magazine – A solid resource for volunteering, working and studying abroad, Verge features numerous blogs and articles on their website as well as a comprehensive directory of programs. (*www.vergemagazine.com*)

Fellowship for Intentional Communities – The FIC runs a directory that lists intentional communities that travellers can visit for anywhere from a day to months, years or even permanently. Intentional communities are planned residential communities in which like-minded people come together to live out their common vision and lifestyle. There are many opportunities to learn hands-on practical skills, attend spiritual teachings and live an alternative lifestyle. (*www.ic.org*)

Travel-living – The Mindful Word's travel-living section offers a number of helpful articles on travel-living, an alternative way to travel that's a cross between travelling and living: working flexible telecommute jobs, volunteering and getting to know a culture by spending lots of time living in one place before moving on. (*www.travel-living.com*)

Retreat Finder – Whether you're looking for a relaxing Yoga getaway or want to learn Buddhism, you can find any retreat-related event on this site. (*www.retreatfinder.com*)

Slow Travel – This site is focused on a different approach to travel where more time is spent in one place, deeply getting to know it rather than dashing from one place to the next. Read trip reports and detailed information on vacation rentals, restaurants and activities from other slow travellers. (*www.slowtrav.com*)

Reviews

TripAdvisor – With such a large base of users TripAdvisor has grown into the go-to resource for finding travel reviews. You can never really know the intention of a reviewer, but if you find enough reviews singing praises of a place or trashing it, it can be a good assessment of a place. (*www.tripadvisor.com*)

The Backpacker – A reviews site similar to TripAdvisor but focused on hostels. (*www.thebackpacker.com*)

Learning Languages

Pimsleur – An effective method for learning a language quickly, the Pimsleur approach to learning is auditory-based, in which learners listen and respond to audio recordings. (*www.pimsleur.com*)

Transitions Abroad – A comprehensive resource for finding language schools all around the world. It's also a handy resource for working, teaching, studying, volunteering and living abroad. (*www.transitionsabroad.com/ listings/ study/ language*)

Live Mocha – Online language learning site that hooks language learners up with native speakers. (*livemocha.com*)

Computer software and apps – Programs like Rosetta Stone and Anki, and apps like DuoLingo and Innovative Language are effective and convenient to use. Learning a few words a day on your mobile is a great way to building up a strong vocabulary. These tools can help you do that and most are free! (*www.rosettastone.com; ankisrs.net; www.duolingo.com; www.innovativelanguage.com*)

Visa Information

Project Visa – Learn how to get visas for different countries on this helpful database. (*www.projectvisa.com*)

Travel Gear

REI – This U.S.-based retailer offers a great selection of travel and outdoor gear along with top-notch customer service and a 100 per cent satisfaction guaranteed return policy. (*www.rei.com*)
Camping World – Choose from a wide range of camping and RV gear. (*www.campingworld.com*)
Rand McNally – A trusted source for maps, atlases and GPS accessories. (*www.randmcnally.com*)
Amazon Travel – Find just about everything else for travelling. Amazon also makes the Kindle, a great alternative to paper books for saving space in your luggage. (*www.amazon.com/Travel*)

Health

WHO International Travel and Health – Information and advice on diseases, vaccines, health risks, precautions and more. (*www.who.int/ith*)
CDC Travel Health – This site provides travel health notices, advice on vaccines, medicine, a disease directory and more useful information (*www.cdc.gov/travel*)

Weather

The Weather Channel – Find detailed hourly or long-term forecasts. Another handy function is searching the historical weather statistics of a place to see what the weather is usually like at a certain time of year. (*www.weather.com*)

Travel Insurance

World Nomads – This company specializes in providing flexible travel insurance. They provide coverage for medication, evacuation, 24-hour emergency assistance and many adventure activities for residents of over 150 countries. (*www.worldnomads.com*)

Allianz – Another option for travel insurance from the world's largest insurance company. (*www.allianztravelinsurance.com*)

Travel Credit Cards

Chase Sapphire Preferred – This card gives you 2x points on all travel and restaurant purchases and 1x points on everything else you buy. They'll also give you 40,000 bonus points if you spend $3,000 in the first three months. (*creditcards.chase.com*)

Barclaycard Arrival World Mastercard – On this card you also earn 2x points on travel and restaurants and 1x on other purchases. There's no annual fee and they'll give you 20,000 bonus miles if you spend $1,000 in the first 90 days. (*www.barclaycardarrival.com/arrival-travel*)

Travel Blogs

Matador Network – This travel site features an extensive array of travel blogs on all different topics. They also run an online university to teach you travel writing, photography and filmmaking. (*www.matadornetwork.com*)

Tripoto – A different kind of travel blog, Tripoto lets users post their trips then the site maps out the specific itinerary, directions and costs, giving readers a good amount of detail to plan out their trips. (*www.tripoto.com*)

CONTACTS

_____

_____

_____

_____

_____

_____

_____

_____

_____

_____

_____

_____

_____

_____

_____

_____

_____

_____

_____

_____

_____

_____

CONTACTS

_____

_____

_____

_____

_____

_____

_____

_____

_____

_____

_____

_____

_____

_____

_____

_____

_____

_____

_____

_____

CONTACTS

_____

_____

_____

_____

_____

_____

_____

_____

_____

_____

_____

_____

_____

_____

_____

_____

_____

_____

_____

_____

_____

_____

IN CASE OF EMERGENCY

Name:	
Gender:	
Birth date:	
Primary language(s):	
Passport #:	
Phone:	
Email:	
Address:	
Blood type:	
Medical conditions:	
Medications:	
Vaccinations:	
Allergies:	
Additional info:	
Emergency contact:	
Phone:	
Email:	
Family doctor:	
Phone:	
Email:	
Insurance company:	
Policy #:	
Phone:	
Other:	

Looking for some inspiration for your next journey? Want to learn all about mindful tourism? Visit The Mindful Word's travel-living section at www.travel-living.com.

Browse our book shop for more journals and other books at www.themindfulword.org/book-shop.

Made in the USA
San Bernardino, CA
04 January 2015